MW00364221

THE LIFE AND TIMES OF
MILTON H. ERICKSON, M.D.

THE MASTER WOUNDED HEALER

THE LIFE AND TIMES OF

MILTON H. ERICKSON, M.D.

THE MASTER WOUNDED HEALER

A Legacy Book by

John C. Hughes, D.C.

HUGHES PUBLISHING

LAS VEGAS, NV

THE LIFE AND TIMES OF
MILTON H. ERICKSON, M.D.

Hughes Publishing
8436 Squaw Valley Avenue
Las Vegas, NV 89128

This book is dedicated to the genius of Milton H. Erickson, the foremost practitioner of hypnosis in the twentieth-century, who was an outstanding innovator, distinguished clinician, and the leading creator of the modern view of hypnosis as a discipline and therapy.

Into each life some confusion should come; also some enlightenment. And my voice goes everywhere with you, and changes into the voice of your parents, your teachers, your playmates and the voices of the wind and of the rain.

Milton H. Erickson, M.D.

CONTENTS

Milton H. Erickson

1901 – 1980

Clark Hull - Milton Erickson's academic mentor

1884 - 1952

PREFACE

The extant literature on Milton H. Erickson, including his own numerous writings, is enormous in its sheer bulk. However, almost all of it consists of descriptions and critiques of his methods, techniques and concepts, and case histories of his patients. There is no standard biography and only a small amount of biographical matter in the many books about him. Edmonston in *The Induction of Hypnosis* (New York, 1986) has one page on Erickson's life, followed by 19 pages of his techniques and results. Jay Haley in his selections from Erickson's papers, published under the title *Advance Techniques of Hypnosis and Therapy* (New York 1967), provides some material on Erickson's life and career. Additional biographical data can be found in Haley's 1973 work, *Uncommon Therapy,* W. W. Norton, New York. With the exception of the recently published family memoir *Milton H. Erickson, M.D., An American Healer*, edited by Betty Alice Erickson, M.S. and Bradford Keeney, Ph.D. (Ringling Rocks Press 2006) there is no standard biography of Erickson and only a small amount of biographical matter in the numerous books treating of him. That need motivated me to publish this concise biography of *The Life and Times of Milton H. Erickson, M.D., The Master Wounded Healer.*

An earlier version of this biography was published in a much longer work *The World's Greatest Hypnotists* (University Press of America, 1996). Understandably the benchmark for a biography is its accuracy. This book meets that criterion. How can I make such a bold statement, you ask? Let me explain:

In a book review published in The Milton H. Erickson Foundation Newsletter, (Fall 1997) Erickson's daughter Roxanna Erickson Klein, Ph.D., R.N. said in reference to my history of hypnotism ". . . The most contemporary of the hypnotists identified in this work is Milton H. Erickson. Two chapters are dedicated to his life and his work. For this review, his widow, Elizabeth, was asked to read these two chapters carefully, and search for errors. Although one relatively inconsequential error was found (Erickson fell ill with polio after high school, not between his junior and senior year as reported) both she and I were very positively impressed with the comprehensiveness and overall accuracy of the author's account. . . ."

John C. Hughes, D.C.

Las Vegas, NV

FOREWORD

John Hughes has done it again! He has written a book that captures the essence of Milton Erickson, a central figure in the modern history of hypnotism. Dr. Hughes is without a doubt the one author who combines his extensive knowledge of the history of hypnotism with his superb and articulate ability to bring its characters to life again.

Besides many articles and books on the history of hypnosis, John Hughes wrote the encyclopedia article on hypnotism for the 1998 Grolier edition of The New Book of Knowledge.

In this book Hughes shows us the life of a remarkable man, who was beset with persistent pain and debilitating physical problems from the age of seventeen to the very end of his life. Despite constant pain, Erickson persevered and developed innovative therapeutic approaches, using hypnosis for the healing of his patients.

Erickson was a psychiatrist, trained in the traditional way at the time, who realized that it was crucial in the healing of problems to be aware of the patient's uniqueness and individuality, more than the use of any particular technique.

Erickson was versatile and used hypnosis in diverse ways, including standard hypnotic inductions and suggestions. I point this out because of a prevalent misconception that Erickson seldom made use of standard hypnotic inductions and used metaphors, story-telling, and indirect approaches as his primary modes of treatment. Robert Pearson, who worked with Erickson, said at most metaphor and indirect hypnosis accounted for no more than a fifth of his hypnotic work. His flexibility and fearless use of innovative techniques made him the pioneer and superb healer that he was. John Hughes makes this abundantly clear.

Erickson's later physical deterioration, despite his earlier ability to cure many of his own problems using visualization and self-hypnosis, shows us an enfeebled man in great pain, who unselfishly persevered and used his energy for his patients and students. He generously gave of himself up to the very end.

I found Erickson's use of the subconscious mind relevant in terms of my own work. I often used hypnosis to uncover forgotten memories in the healing process. As a psychiatrist, Erickson was concerned with retrieving and identifying a patient's core emotions from early life. He realized that traumas from earlier in life that had been buried by repression, needed to be brought to the surface.

Hughes shows how Erickson's view of the unconscious mind (a term Erickson preferred to the subconscious) differed from Sigmund Freud. I found this very interesting, reflecting and contrasting the older view with a more modern one. Erickson also had, as Hughes states, a more "generous" view of the person and his ability to live in our world with its restrictions than Freud did.

This insightful book gives the reader a comprehensive, yet concise, understanding of the life and work of a compassionate and remarkable man that many considered a genius.

No one can dispute his great contribution to the use of hypnosis in healing and bringing hypnotism into the mainstream of acceptable therapeutic approaches.

I found this book extremely interesting, readable and informative. Thank you, Dr. Hughes for *Milton H. Erickson, M.D. The Master Wounded Healer*––this excellent biography has performed a distinct service to the field of hypnotism and to the history of psychotherapy.

Edith Fiore, Ph.D. Clinical Psychologist (Ret.)

Sarasota, Florida

THE ARRIVAL OF
MILTON H. ERICKSON

The 1920s were a time of indecision about, and opposition to, the validity and usefulness of hypnotism as a therapy. On the one hand, there was an intense public interest—shared to some extent by medical professionals—in finding out more about how the human mind works and what could be done through it to overcome disorders of the body.

On the other hand there was a general skepticism and impatience on the public's part that denied innovative approaches an adequate trial, and among the professionals a hesitancy and distrust of anything that did not fit into their textbook preconceptions. In addition to William McDougall's *Outline of Abnormal Psychology,* published in 1926, which derived in part from the seminal work of the British psychologist Halse Rivers in diagnosing shell-shock and other psychic traumas of front-line soldiers in World War I, there were many books—by popular writers such as Camille Flammarion—that kept hypnotism and the subconscious mind in the public eye. Yet there were very few doctors offering hypnosis as a therapy, and few places where medical students or practicing physicians could seek professional training in hypnotism. Nor would this state of affairs alter materially for an entire generation.

Nevertheless, the advent of a new and scientifically sound hypnosis as a therapy was obfuscated in the early 1920s, while the Couéism fad was at its height. (The French pharmacist Emile Coué who became famous for his autosuggestion formula, "Every day in every way, I am getting better and better.")

At the University of Wisconsin Clark L. Hull, who held the chair of psychology, began holding seminars on hypnotism with both graduate and undergraduate students. Hypnotism had interested him throughout his long academic career—he was then in his late fifties—and though he strongly doubted that hypnosis had much medical value, he was eager to determine whether it could be pinned down in its various modes into textbook categories.

Among the students to whom Hull gave investigative assignments was one who was destined to be the greatest hypnotist of the twentieth-century, and to rank with the most eminent of the past. He was Milton H. Erickson, whose life history had some remarkable points of similarity to Hull's. The latter had originally been educated as a mining engineer, but after being partially disabled by an attack of polio, he turned to a career in psychology because it was less demanding physically.

Erickson was born December 5, 1901 in Aurum, Nevada, a mining camp that is now a ghost town. His father had been a farmer, and shortly after his son was born he gave up mining to return to Wisconsin to resume farming. Erickson's ambition as a youth was to become a farmer too—a modern, up-to-date one. At seventeen he had already published an article in a national magazine on why young people did not want to stay on farms and what could be done to persuade them to do so. Then, just after finishing high school in 1918, he was stricken with polio which left him almost totally paralyzed. Through a combination of mental imagery and stubborn determination, Erickson recovered sufficiently to go to the university and train to become a medical doctor, the career he chose as an alternative to farming for which he no longer had the physical strength. Erickson realized that his recovery from a state of helplessness had been largely due to his having developed the ability to self-induce a trance state (i.e., self-hypnosis) in which he imaged step-by-step each stage of regaining his body's mobility. He was thus readily drawn to Hull's classes on hypnotism, and the shared elements in their lives made them at first highly responsive to each other. In the summer of 1923, with Hull's encouragement, Erickson carried out a number of experiments that sought to investigate the nature of hypnosis, the processes of induction, and the relative roles of the hypnotist and the subject, including which was the more important in trance development. His findings give rise to lively debates in Hull's seminars that fall, and it was soon clear to him that there was little, if any, common ground between him and his mentor. This recognition moved Erickson to commence a new special investigative project of his own that winter, which led him to conclude that the controlling factor in hypnosis was the subject's individuality and how it interplayed with the suggestions of the hypnotist. This was in agreement with his own experience of introspective self-hypnosis.

Although Erickson summarized his findings in two papers, he did not publish them at the time, for they went against Hull's conviction of the absolute priority of the hypnotist in the induction and facilitation of hypnosis. To Hull, the subconscious mind of the subject was a blank tablet on which the hypnotist could imprint whatever commands he wished. Erickson strongly felt this to be an erroneous concept, but since he was at the beginning of his professional career, he felt he could not afford publicly to oppose or offend Hull, who was becoming an authority to whom all deferred in the field of hypnotism. Thus Erickson remained silent, though he gradually dissociated himself from Hull's further researches, which were soon transferred to Yale, where he was appointed to the Sterling Chair of Psychology. In that position he was, from the late 1920s to mid-century, the foremost figure—albeit a lonely one—in American hypnotherapy. His book *Hypnosis and Suggestibility: An Experimental Approach*, published in 1933, set a standard of scientific control and statistical verification of hypnotic phenomena that even now is a model for the profession. Yet he largely abandoned his own work in hypnotism after the publication of the book, leaving it to others to put its central philosophy into practice. That, unfortunately, was still a rigid insistence that the subject did not contribute in any way to the hypnotic process or its outcome. It was a position that would block any further broad advances in hypnotherapy for a third of the century.

From 1933 on, Hull devoted his energies and abilities to an attempt to quantify the primary laws of psychology, as he conceived them to be, into a neo-behaviorist scheme of things, on the model of Newtonian physics. From these primary laws, he argued, all individual behavior, however complex, could be derived under a set of secondary laws, together with social and group behavior in all their variations. He devised several mathematical equations to express these laws, which he published in 1943, in his book *Principles of Behavior*. For a decade beyond his death in 1952, this work was a Bible of psychological theory and practice, seemingly assuring Hull a niche among the immortals of science. Then in the 1960s, almost overnight, his fame and influence faded as the impractical and untenable nature of much of his premise became increasingly evident.

Today, Clark Hull is remembered by few, even among professionals, and most of those few blame him for having held back the development of modern hypnotherapy with his failed numerical straitjacketing of the human psyche.

Milton Erickson, however, held a more generous view of his academic mentor in hypnotism, recalling how Hull had encouraged and directed his youthful interest in the discipline. He also valued the statistical solidity and scientific respectability that Hull's landmark *Hypnosis and Suggestibility: An Experimental Approach* gave to American hypnotherapy when it was sadly lacking in both. In addition, Hull's university seminars on hypnotism had been important since they took place in a time of rapidly declining interest on the part of professional medicine.

Erickson's balanced assessment of Hull's contribution to hypnotherapy is probably in line with what is likely to be the eventual judgment of medical historians. Though Erickson and a host of practitioners after him went far beyond Hull, the fact remains that without the scientific credibility he provided, it might have been another fifty years or more before hypnotism was again used in therapy. And the maturing of Erickson's own genius and attainment of pre-eminence in hypnotherapy would have had to surmount even greater obstacles than the many he overcame in his climb to fame and recognition.

Many of these obstacles were connected with his physical health. He had a near-fatal attack of polio at seventeen, and going back even further, there were physical deficiencies that hindered his early education. He was tone-deaf and red-green color-blind; he had a severe dyslexia which vanished in an instant flash of visual illumination when trying to follow his frustrated teacher's explanation that the characters *M* and *3* were not the same. This occurred when he was in either first or second grade. From that moment he had no further problem with learning to read except that until he was in his second year at high school he was unable to find words in their alphabetical sequence in the dictionary and had to keep turning the pages until he found the word he was looking for. Then, just as suddenly as the reading disability had disappeared, this one also vanished in a flash of insight.

Recalling these sudden illuminations some sixty years later, Erickson concluded that they were the result of his having self-induced, without realizing it, a trance state in which the intense concentration on his reading limitations brought about their elimination. Whether or not that was so, there can be no question about the role of concentration, imagery and self-hypnosis in Erickson's recovery from polio. From a state of total paralysis, and a partial loss of his speech faculty, he regained within eleven months the ability to walk, though still needing crutches, and was again able to speak clearly. His recovery enabled him in 1920 to work at a sit-down job in a cannery all summer to earn money for college. He entered medical school at the University of Wisconsin that fall.

Long afterward, Erickson told his second wife that there was some physical therapy involved in his recovery. A local practical nurse treated him with hot packs and massage, and by moving the paralyzed limbs, while also motivating him to move them on his own. This was essentially the same method later employed by Sister Kenny in Australia, which aroused the fierce opposition of the medical profession. Nevertheless, Erickson believed it was the depth of concentration and clarity of imaging that was the principal factor in his overcoming the extreme degree of incapacitating paralysis he had suffered.

His hearing, which had been only average, became exceptionally sharp and sensitive as his body sought to compensate for its loss of mobility; and he availed himself of this heightened auditory faculty to start to identify every sound in the house and all that he could hear from outdoors. Soon he could accurately determine who was making what sound, and what activity and mood it denoted. Next, he used his eyesight, which also appears to have acquired a heightened acuteness, to scan the windows closely, while he sat in bed and also in the rocking chair into which it shortly became possible to lift himself. This intense focusing on the windows, and concentration on the idea of reaching them and looking out, induced an auto-hypnotic state in which he was actually starting to rock the chair and very gradually slide it toward the window. He concentrated on recalling the movements of his hands, feet, fingers and toes in grasping tools and utensils, in walking and climbing trees, and visualized performing the same actions again. Before long he was indeed renewing those motions. From watching closely his baby sister learning to walk and to balance herself, he visualized himself doing the same all over again—and was soon doing it.

He was, however, still having to use crutches through his freshman year at the university, and had a general feeling of physical weakness. Determining to toughen himself through a stretch of outdoor living, he set out in June 1921 on what he assured his parents would be a two-week canoe trek down the Wisconsin River and back. He was actually gone ten weeks, going from the Wisconsin into the Mississippi, and down that river to beyond St. Louis, then back up against the current in both streams; a total of twelve hundred miles. On his return he was in much stronger physical condition, with powerful shoulder muscles developed through strenuous paddling, and again was able to ride a bicycle. He now discarded the crutches, though he continued to carry a cane and occasionally used it for balancing. In addition he had met a great variety of people and learned much about conducting himself in many different situations.

Yet there was a physical price to be paid for these gains. Erickson's right shoulder muscles never regained the strength of those in his left shoulder; and to keep the left shoulder from becoming markedly higher and giving him a disfigured appearance, he stood long hours in front of a mirror, twisting himself until the two shoulders were approximately level. That, however, resulted in a severely twisted spine that had already been damaged by the polio. This would cause severe problems in later life. For the time being, however, Erickson had achieved a nearly normal physical appearance and capability of movement.

After his investigations into hypnotism under Hull in his senior year, he went on to postgraduate medical school at Wisconsin and qualified in 1928, at the age of twenty-six, for his medical and master's degree in psychology. His first internship in general medicine was at the Colorado General Hospital, and in psychiatry at the nearby Colorado Psychopathic Hospital where he worked under Dr. Franklin Ebaugh, one of the more noted psychiatrists of the 1920s.

After a year at these Colorado institutions, Erickson was appointed assistant physician at the Rhode Island State Hospital for Mental Diseases, where he did some intensive studies in the relationship of mental deficiencies to family and environmental factors. His findings resulted in seven papers being published in professional journals, which started to bring him into notice and led to a better paying tenure at the State Hospital in Worcester, Massachusetts, where in four years (1930-34) he progressed from junior physician to Chief Research Psychiatrist. It was at Worcester that he first started to use hypnosis extensively as a therapeutic tool. The hospital staff was opposed to this, fearing that hypnosis was potentially dangerous to sanity, and he had to overcome this hostility through carefully controlled experiments in which he demonstrated its safety. His resulting paper, published in 1932 in the *Journal of Abnormal and Social Psychology*, was a significant first step toward the wider professional utilization of hypnosis in medical practice.

While Erickson was thus advancing in his career, his personal life was unhappy. In his first year of postgraduate medical study, at twenty-three, he had married, and by the early 1930s was raising a family of three children. This was a heavy burden on him with his still relatively low earnings. In hindsight, he realized that early marriage had been a serious mistake on his part. The focusing on himself that had been necessary for him to overcome his paralysis had resulted in his failing to develop adequate social and personal relationships with others. He retained a naiveté and immaturity of judgment in the areas of loving and caring that ill fitted him for marriage. After his divorce in 1934, in which he obtained custody of the children, he determined to seek a better understanding of all the things he had been deficient in, and to apply this painfully gained knowledge in his professional practice. In the 1940s and 1950s he was the first to work with families to bring about healing of shattered relationships. Erickson received an appointment in 1934 as Director of Psychiatric Research at the Wayne County General Hospital in Eloise, Michigan, a Detroit suburb. Five years later this position was expanded to cover Psychiatric Training as well; he was associate professor of psychiatry at the Wayne State University College of Medicine and professor in the graduate school. Concurrently, he was a visiting professor of clinical psychology at Michigan State University, in East Lansing. He remained a total of fourteen years at the Wayne County institution. It was at Eloise that Erickson started to attain true maturity both as a person and as a healer.

A prime factor in this further growth was his meeting Elizabeth Moore, whom he married in 1936. She became his fellow researcher and inspiration, a step-mother to the three children he already had, and mother of five more she would bear. Without her steadying and strengthening presence, Erickson could not have become the dominant leader of the hypnotherapy revival in the 1960s and 1970s.

At the time of his second marriage he was thirty-four and physically still vigorous and active, though the limp on his right side that he never fully overcame was becoming more pronounced and he now had to use a cane all the time. However, he could walk surprisingly long distances, and he still had powerful shoulder muscles.

His physical deterioration started in 1947, at age forty-five, when he was knocked off his bicycle by a dog and suffered extensive skin abrasions. Given a tetanus antitoxin injection, he developed a severe reaction from which he had great difficulty recovering. In particular he seemed no longer able to tolerate the chill and dampness of the Michigan winter. A friend and former Detroit psychiatrist, Dr. John Larson, who was Superintendent of the Arizona State Hospital at Phoenix, invited Erickson to come and join his staff. With his family, Erickson moved to Phoenix in the early summer of 1948, and in the warm dry climate his health improved markedly. He also found an outlet for his energies in helping Dr. Larson institute numerous progressive changes at the hospital, which had been run in an outmoded and obsolete manner.

In the spring of 1949, political opposition forced Larson's resignation, and Erickson also decided to leave the hospital staff and go into private practice. He was ill again twice within a few months, apparently from allergic reactions to the desert environment with its sand and dust. To reduce exposure to them, he set up his office in the home he had bought in Phoenix, so he did not have to travel to and from another location.

His condition then seems to have become stabilized, until 1953 when he suffered what was diagnosed at the time as a second attack of polio, but is now believed to have been an episode of post-polio syndrome, traceable to the original attack twenty-four years earlier. There were further episodes of this through the remaining twenty-seven years of Erickson's life;

and while these were not as severe as the first one in 1953, each caused a further muscle impairment until in the end, as will be seen further on, he was reduced to virtually total invalidism.

It was while first coming under this weight of steadily worsening physical debility that Erickson heightened his initial prominence in the hypnotherapeutic field. He had already, while at his post in Michigan, attracted the notice of Dr. Margaret Mead, who consulted him in 1939 regarding the spontaneous trances of the native dancers she had filmed in Bali. They collaborated during World War II on still classified government projects assessing the Japanese character and the effectiveness of Nazi propaganda. At this time he also became the associate editor of the *Journal of Diseases of the Nervous System*, and was interviewed several times by newspapers and radio stations, as well as national publications such as *Life* and *This Week*. In addition he frequently spoke to civic and youth groups, and at graduations, taking advantage of all these opportunities to promote a wider public understanding of hypnotism.

The response was still slow and meager, but the seed was being sown that would bear abundant harvest later on. In the decade of the 1950s Erickson became a nationally known figure, featured in the news media and consulted by famous athletes, the U.S. military, and the airline industry for improved performance by both individuals and groups. Even though the emphasis was still mainly on the psychology involved, and his masterly application of it through his psychiatric techniques, the fact that hypnotism was the most important of them was finally getting across to the public and to some portion of the medical profession. A giant step forward to greater acceptance of hypnotherapy was the founding, in 1957, largely by Erickson's initiative, of the American Society of Clinical Hypnosis, with him as its first president and first editor of its Journal. He was the president for two years, and editor for ten years.

All this came about despite his physical disabilities that grew worse every year, as also did the demands on his time and strength. By the late 1950s invitations to speak and demonstrate his inimitable techniques to professional groups across the country and abroad were coming at such a rate that Erickson was away from home for at least a week every month. And still his greatest attainments, in the sense of developing a coherent philosophy of what he sought for his patients and how he achieved it, lay ahead of him. They would make the 1960s and 1970s a period when Erickson towered over the fields of psychiatry and hypnotherapy, laying new foundations and opening new approaches that will occupy his successors far into this twenty-first century. We will now take up the panorama of those two epochal decades.

ERICKSON
THE MASTER WOUNDED HEALER

At the Seventh Congress of the International Society of Hypnotists held in 1976, Milton Erickson was the first recipient of its newly created Benjamin Franklin Gold Medal award for the highest level of achievement in the theory and practice of hypnotism. He was cited as an outstanding innovator, distinguished clinician, and the leading creator of the modern view of hypnosis as a discipline and therapy. This was followed in July, 1977 by the publication of a special issue of the American Journal of Clinical Hypnosis (of which he had been the founder and first editor two decades earlier) in honor of his seventy-fifth birthday. It included a tribute by Margaret Mead, who was the first figure of national prominence in psychology to recognize Erickson's genius.

Now, halfway through the seventh decade of his life, Milton Erickson was known and looked up to everywhere in the Western world as the premier figure in the field of hypnotherapy. Though he had given up active practice and was totally confined to his wheelchair, he was still avidly sought out by those in the rising generation of psychotherapists who hoped to be his disciples and to carry to new heights his legacy of creative and innovative healing through hypnosis. Some of these new aspirants to Erickson's heritage, notably Ernest Rossi and Jeffrey Zeig, have risen to prominence since his death on March 25, 1980, at the age of seventy-eight. Yet there is still no general agreement among professionals as to exactly what constitutes an Ericksonian approach to therapy. There are many who say they are doing—or trying to do—what Erickson did, but no one is following him exactly on the path he took.

Indeed, it is hardly possible that they could, for Milton Erickson was a law unto himself, a master innovator who early in his career had understood that he would have to go beyond textbooks and theories. They were the indispensable foundation, but what he built on them was based on his own best insights and judgment. He had come to trust them through years of experience, from which he learned that he had to approach each case on its own merits. No two patients were alike. What worked with one may not work with another. At the same time, there were certain general principles, mainly of common sense, that could usually be relied upon to produce results. Effective treatment involved determining the best mix and application of these principles to each individual case.

Erickson did not always succeed. Though he never revealed any scorecard of successes and failures, he freely admitted that he had encountered many patients he could not help. Some were simply not hypnotizable and offered no other access to their twisted inner complexes. Some who could be hypnotized lacked the inner wish to be helped. An important part of any therapist's practice, he taught his pupils, was learning how to detect that a patient could not be helped. His techniques for doing that were, however, very much his own, and not easily adaptable—if at all—for use by others who were not at ease with his often very unconventional approaches. Whether for diagnosis or treatment, those approaches spanned a very wide range, broader in scope than those of any of Erickson's predecessors. He himself never sought to systematize them—he avoided systems of any sort—but their often dazzling variety can be roughly grouped under the headings below.

To a great extent Erickson employed indirect suggestion, confusion, puzzlement, and metaphor. "I try," he would say, "to get the patient to learn about himself, in an unstructured way." Erickson's suggestions and leading questions—at which he was as expert as any trial lawyer—concentrated the patient's attention to the point where he or she would enter the hypnotic state without the customary induction ritual. He utilized traditional induction procedures too, very capably, when the occasion called for them, but they were not his primary tools.

To say that Erickson often employed metaphor is to oversimplify his vast assortment of techniques of analogy and anecdote. He was a charismatic story-teller, whether he was addressing an audience or a patient. Few could resist becoming wholly wrapped up in his tales, which often seemed to have no relation at all to the patient's situation or problem. They had a very distinct purpose however, which was to open up the patient's mind on both conscious and subconscious levels to what was wrong with him or her, and the need to take definite steps to change the anomalous behavior.

When the situation called for it, Erickson could be extremely authoritative, issuing preemptive commands instead of softly spoken suggestions. He knew when to employ shock techniques to compel patients to make choices instead of evading them. Sometimes he enabled those with bad habits to overcome them through even greater indulgence, until they grasped just how harmful and self-destructive those habits were.

Erickson was particularly effective in situations where he could make use of his talent for creating high drama, in which the patient played the leading role. He did not write the script, but he provided the setting and the strategy, leaving it up to the patient to devise—aided by his suggestions—the tactics to play out the drama to a successful conclusion. To critics who charged him with being manipulative, he countered that all psychotherapy was manipulative in one way or another. What mattered was the objective and the values involved.

With Erickson, the values were always those of traditional morality, softened only to the extent that common sense and sensitivity to suffering demanded. He was not religious in any church-going sense, though he had experienced mystical states at various times in his life. He believed very strongly that there was a right way for people to behave, with consideration and respect, toward themselves and others. If a religious conviction or affiliation helped anyone to cultivate proper behavior, that was well and good, but he never relied on or employed religious motivations in seeking to effect beneficial change in a patient.

One criticism of Erickson was that when inculcating a sense of values into patients, he tended to lecture them in the fashion of a moralizing Dutch uncle. Some resisted this and claimed it was demeaning, but the majority appears to have accepted it and it seems to have achieved its purpose. Perhaps his speech rhythm, which was about seventy-five words a minute (half that of most people) and resembled the intonation of a priest or lector reading a text aloud, acted as an induction mode, facilitating a trance-like absorption in and acceptance of what he was saying.

So strong was the impression that Erickson's voice made on his listeners that it made his posthypnotic suggestions more emphatic and effective. "My voice will go with you," he would say, and the memory of it would reinforce the suggestions within the patient's subconscious. However, it was not his custom to make hypnotic suggestions overt; usually they were concealed inside the anecdotal story or other narrative device he used to concentrate the patient's attention.

As a psychiatrist, Erickson was concerned with retrieving and identifying a patient's core emotions from early life, and he made very effective use of hypnosis for this purpose. He realized, perhaps more clearly than most practitioners, that the validity of such retrievals depended on how much they were influenced by the patient's eagerness to please and satisfy the therapist. In many cases the memories brought up were not of real events, but what the patient thought the therapist wanted and expected. With this in mind Erickson worded his questions to patients in hypnosis in ways that tended to elicit truthful answers. He was careful not to prejudge the responses, but he had usually formed a pretty accurate idea of what the patient might be concealing from what had come out in pre-induction questioning.

Therapists who attended his seminars and workshops often despaired of ever being able to match his flexibility and eclecticism in their own practice. They realized that these were qualities in which he excelled uniquely, and that this was the key to his preeminence. Patients quickly realized that they were being treated by a learned person who was at the head of his profession, and this made them feel special also.

On a philosophic level, Erickson did not subscribe to Freud's belief in the incompatibility of human biological urges and civilization. This, to him, seemed to fly in the face of the common sense perception that the vast majority of people were able to live normally with those urges inside the constraints that civilization imposes. The goal of psychotherapy, as he saw it, was to free those persons shackled by attitudes of rigidity and timidity that prevented them from functioning usefully within civilized society. For this purpose, hypnosis—which he once defined as any state of absorption in which the attention could be concentrated on a single thought or idea—was by far the most effective means. It unlocked the vast hidden powers of the unconscious, a term Erickson preferred to the subconscious.

Whatever the name, he looked on that postulated region of the psyche (the unconscious) as a source of power and strength, a reservoir of resources to be drawn on by the conscious surface personality for its better and more healthful functioning. This was diametrically opposite to Freud's view, which regarded the subconscious with suspicion, as a hiding place of malignant memories and impulses. Erickson, though he had no illusions about people's propensity to deviousness and trickery, had a more generous conception of human nature than did Freud. This optimism helped him to take an active interest in each patient and to convey a belief that relief or cure was possible and attainable.

At the same time, he did not believe there were limitless powers of healing in the human unconscious. There was a boundary to everything, and the human body—marvelously constructed as it was, with capabilities of resilience and recovery of which conventional medicine had no conception—still had its ultimate design limits beyond which it could not be sustained. The amplest evidence of this was his own steadily deteriorating physical condition. He helped and frequently healed others; himself he could help less and less as time went on, and nothing he did would much longer sustain his increasingly crippled body. Erickson was in fact the epitome of the archetypal "wounded healer," who appears in the mythology and folklore of peoples around the globe. The archetype is present even in the Christian figure of the divine Jesus, who on the cross is mocked by the crowd shouting, "He saved others, himself he cannot save." Facing up to the reality that his physical deterioration was irreversible, Erickson nevertheless called on his own inner resources to allow him to continue helping others as long as possible. In spite of pain that became nearly constant, and virtually total loss of mobility, he lived into his seventy-ninth year and to the very end was still active in many ways. This was a medical miracle that owed very little to conventional medical therapy, though he made use of it to the extent that he felt it was of value.

Erickson's physical breakdown intensified steadily from about 1967 on, even while he was attaining the peak of his fame and recognition. The once powerful shoulder muscles weakened to the point that he needed both hands to lift spoons, knives, and forks when eating. Walking, even with a cane, became too exhausting by 1969, when he had to give up traveling. A year later he moved into another home in Phoenix which had been remodeled for wheelchair living. Even so, he continued to do research, write papers, do organizational work and editing, and see patients. By 1974 he had to give that up, as with further loss of cheek and tongue muscle control he could no longer wear dentures or enunciate as clearly as before. He also had to give up much of his reading, as he could no longer maintain eye-focus for an extended length of time.

Yet he did not become totally inactive professionally. He was increasingly in demand for teaching sessions at his home. At first, in the mid-1970s, he was able to do these both mornings and afternoons, five days a week, then in the afternoons only, and finally only on four days a week. So many were the requests to attend these sessions that, when he died on a Tuesday evening in late March 1980, his teaching schedule was filled through the end of the year, and there were applications that would have extended it through the following year.

Through collaboration with his favorite disciples Ernest Rossi and Jeffrey Zeig, Erickson was able to continue contributing to the professional literature on hypnotherapy. The demand for papers by him—satisfied to some extent by reprinting earlier ones from as far back as forty years that had attracted little notice on their first appearance—had grown enormously since the publication in 1973 of Jay Haley's *Uncommon Therapy: the Psychiatric Techniques of Milton H. Erickson, M.D.* It was this book that first made a large sector of the medical and psychiatric professions, which had not previously paid much notice to the acclaim Erickson had been steadily gaining from his peers, more fully aware of the breakthrough character of his methods. As Mesmer and the Nancy School had done in their centuries,

Erickson in his century lifted hypnotism to previously unattained levels as a therapy, laying the foundation for still further gains in the century ahead. And as had been the case with Mesmer and the Nancy School, Erickson's achievements have not been immediately followed by new ones of equal stature. No corpus of hypnotherapeutic theory or practice has appeared that can be identified as strictly Ericksonian, because his unique approach was simply beyond imitation. He set examples and laid down principles that can be built upon, amplified, and further developed, but no matter what the degree or direction of these advances, they inevitably depart from both the spirit and the letter of his approach. To the extent, however, that therapists adhere to his openness and diversity of approach, they can claim to be practicing a form of Ericksonian therapy.

Five years after Erickson's death, D. Cory-don Hammond of the University of Utah School of Medicine, in a symposium at the Tenth Congress of the International Society of Hypnotists, held in Toronto, Canada, delivered an analysis of the varying attempts at following in Erickson's footsteps. Hammond's paper is a valid statement of the Ericksonian legacy and of how it is being handled.

Some of the misinterpretations that Ham-mond described are surprising in light of how clearly Erickson elucidated his techniques in a vast body of writings. For instance, Erickson's entry into self-hypnosis in the diagnostic process, which was on occasion helpful to him in grasping the nature of the patient's problem, has been misunderstood as being his standard method. The harmful result has been training sessions in which aspiring therapists are encouraged to go into hypnosis and trust their unconscious to come up with the esoteric metaphors and paradoxes that Erickson often employed—and to expect such superficial methodology to produce results as positive and lasting as those that he obtained.

That is merely an evasion of the hard work and careful planning that Erickson devoted to each individual case. He had no intention of founding any sort of cult, or of propounding dogmas of either theory or practice. He did believe, because he had seen it proved over and over again, that the results you get are in direct proportion to the effort you put into solving the problem. Some of this misapprehension stemmed from the teaching seminars he conducted in his last years. Because of his increasingly severe physical limitations, they were not formal classes in any sense. He would reminisce informally about a great many cases in his experience and describe in more or less general terms how he treated them. Such narrations often gave the impression of his having achieved literally magical results through very simple means. But he left out the arduous trial and error through which he had arrived at the correct diagnoses and the appropriate techniques of treatment in each case. He made it sound easy because he was no longer up to telling how hard it was. His results were miraculous only to those who did not appreciate their really common sense nature.

Again, many who claim to be Ericksonian in their practice are actually employing only one, or at best a few, of his many approaches. Often it is asserted that the true Ericksonian method is to implant hypnotic suggestion indirectly. Actually he used direct suggestion about as frequently as indirect, but because indirect suggestion had rarely been used and was unknown to many practitioners, he naturally emphasized it in his case histories. Why talk at equal length about what was known already?

Ernest Rossi summed up Erickson's genius as an extreme flexibility in applying whatever was appropriate to the given situation—of knowing when to use what. "It is natural," Rossi said, "when we encounter a genius who does something new (such as indirect suggestion) to jump on that one facet as being the total of what makes a genius. That totally misses the eclecticism that is often a hallmark of geniuses, and certainly was emphatically so with Erickson."

The late Kay Thompson, another therapist familiar with Erickson's work at first hand said, "We simply don't believe in ourselves enough . . . we don't believe we have the power to make the direct approach work for us, as he made it work for him. We chicken out and resort to the indirect approach—and don't do so well with that either—because we lack the belief and skills needed for the direct one. Erickson was successful with both methods because he had fully mastered each."

Again, the later followers of Erickson have made metaphor and story-telling a prime factor in their modes of treatment, even though therapists such as Robert Pearson, who worked with Erickson, have said that at most metaphor accounted for no more than a fifth of his hypnotic work. The misconception here was that Erickson did not trust patients to obey him or follow his directions, so he conveyed suggestions in the form of metaphorical stories that distracted the patient and diffused resistance to what he was instilling. Rather, according to Pearson, Erickson wanted to give his patients time for integrating what they had already been told. Stories were a way of giving that time without boring them. Nor were they mere idle tales, spun on the spur of the moment. Erickson invariably made a direct connection between them and the patient's problem, and was careful in making essential points to that end.

Erickson said that he often spent more time in reviewing the details of each session with a patient than in the sessions themselves. He wrote down everything that was said, and what he planned to say at the next session. It was this exhaustive preparation and reviewing that made his words and actions appear effortless and spontaneous. Many who claim to be his followers, Kay Thompson has charged, think they can do the same simply by entering self-hypnosis and trusting their unconscious to come up with the right words. "They've put nothing into their unconscious, so nothing useful comes out of it," Thompson said. "They don't want to do the painstaking, exhausting work Erickson did." Nor, it would seem, do they want to give their patients the hours of intensive training in developing the hypnotic state that Erickson always provided before he undertook the implantation of therapeutic suggestions. Even with a patient who had previously been hypnotized, he insisted on a minimum of twenty minutes in the hypnotic state before the patient was given appropriate posthypnotic suggestions.

Erickson put the interests of his patients ahead of his own. He gave them sixty minutes out of every hour, rather than the fifty which has become more common in the psychotherapy profession, and even with the onset of inflation in the early 70s his fees never exceeded $40.00 an hour up to the time he gave up private practice. He did not amass monetary wealth, but he left to his family and to his colleagues a legacy of high and strict principles, dedicated application, and a conviction that service to others had a value above all else.

The advancement of modern hypnosis needs to be in accordance with the standards that Milton Erickson set and followed throughout his long professional career.

MILTON H. ERICKSON, M.D.
THE MASTER WOUNDED HEALER

AUTHOR'S NOTES AND REFERENCES

A s stated in the Preface the extant literature on Milton H. Erickson, including his own numerous writings, is enormous in its sheer bulk. However, almost all of it consists of descriptions and critiques of his methods, techniques and concepts, and case histories of his patients. There is no standard biography and only a small amount of biographical matter in the many books about him. Edmonston in *The Induction of Hypnosis* (New York, 1986) has one page on Erickson's life, followed by 19 pages of his techniques and results. Jay Haley in his selections from Erickson's papers, published under the title *Advance Techniques of Hypnosis and Therapy* (New York 1967), provides some material on Erickson's life and career. Additional biographical data can be found in Haley's 1973 work, *Uncommon Therapy*, W. W. Norton, New York. *Milton H. Erickson, M.D., An American Healer*, edited by Betty Alice Erickson and Bradford Keeney, Ringling Rocks Foundation, 2006. This insightful book by Erickson's family members, and people who were close to him, contains several photographs and includes a DVD of a clinical session.

The best summations are Jeffrey K. Zeig's in his *Experiencing Erickson* Brunner/Mazel, New York, 1985; and that of Rossi, Ryan and Sharp in *Healing in Hypnosis,* Irvington Publishers, New York, 1983 based on Milton H. Erickson's seminars, workshops and lectures.

Also helpful are Zeig's *A Teaching Seminar with Milton H. Erickson,* Brunner/Mazel, New York, 1980 and S. Rosen, *My Voice Will Go With you.* All of these cited books provide further extensive references on Erickson's philosophy and work.

Ericksonian Approaches to Hypnosis and Psychotherapy, edited by J. K. Zeig, Brunner/Mazel 1982, has an excellent summation by Jay Haley on Erickson's contribution to therapy. See also, in the same volume, S. Rosen on Erickson's values and philosophy; I. Secter on Erickson's earlier seminars; and C. A. Dammann on Erickson's family therapy.

Two collaborative works by Erickson and Rossi, *Hypnotherapy: An Exploratory Casebook*, Irvington, New York, 1979, and *Experiencing Hypnosis: Therapeutic Approaches to Altered States,* Irvington 1981, provide insight into Erickson's concepts and his applications of them.

A wide range of views on Erickson's enduring significance and importance can be found in the July 1988 (vol. XXXVI, no 3) International Journal of Clinical and Experimental Hypnosis. The entire issue is devoted to transcripts of addresses by prominent speakers in the hypnotherapeutic field, at the 10th Congress of the International Society of Hypnotists, held in Toronto in August 1985. Erickson's eclecticism and avoidance are stressed in the address "Will the Real Milton Erickson Please Stand Up?" by D. Corydon Hammond of the University of Utah School of Medicine.

THE LIFE AND TIMES OF
MILTON H. ERICKSON, M.D.
THE MASTER WOUNDED HEALER

A LEGACY AUDIOBOOK NARRATED BY
JOHN C. HUGHES, D.C.

The Audiobook
is Available Now!

Author
John C. Hughes
personally reads from
this classic selection.

This vivid, revelatory and exhaustively
researched biography is now available as an
audiobook, narrated by the author. It gives
Milton H. Erickson his rightful place as a principal
architect of modern hypnotherapy.

**Order the Audiobook as a
great gift for yourself or a friend.**

John C. Hughes, D.C. is a noted authority on the history
of hypnotism and the author of many books and
articles over his fifty year career. His books include *The
Illustrated History of Hypnotism*, and *The Roots of
Hypnotism in America*. His many articles cover topics
including historical practices, professional ethics and
practice technique. A respected scholar he authored
the encyclopedia article on hypnotism in the New Book
of Knowledge. Hearing this dynamic book in Dr. Hughes
own voice is a rewarding experience you will always
remember.

CPSIA information can be obtained
at www.ICGtesting.com
Printed in the USA
BVHW041639140222
628975BV00008B/197